Down on the Farm in Georgia

A Poetic Memoir

Dwayne Cole

Parson's Porch Books
www.parsonsporchbooks.com

Down on the Farm in Georgia
ISBN: Softcover 978-1-949888-82-9
Copyright © 2019 by Dwayne Cole

All rights reserved. No part of this book may be reproduced or transmitted in any form or by any means, electronic or mechanical, including photocopying, recording, or by any information storage and retrieval system, without permission in writing from the publisher.

Down on the Farm in Georgia

Contents

Dedication 7
Down On The Farm In Georgia 9
Family Data 11
Introduction 13
Buck Creek 15
A Tribute to Father 17
Hugged Home 18
One of My First Memories: Doodlebug 21
Home Maternity Ward 23
Cole Family Barn 24
Joy of Fresh Cut Hay 27
Cotton Picking 29
The Hammer Mill 31
Sorghum Mill 32
Old Gray Mules 34
Blackberry Picking 36
Wild Plums 37
Bobcat Byte 38
Fall Farm Haiku 39
Rolling Country Store 41
Watermelon Thumping Time 42
Dan and Alice 44
Goat Man 46
Gray Fox 49
Why indeed? 52
Fox Limerick 53
Gathering Honey 54
Spearing White Suckers 56

Cherished Memories	57
Chickens	58
Chasing Fireflies	60
Tadpole	61
Front Porch	64
Wendell's Rabbit Boxes	66
Sunday	67
Grandmother	69
Grandfather Cole	70
VW Beetle Drives Away	71
The Day Daddy Died	72
Mother, the Sweetest of All	73
Heaven is Family	74
Robbie, Mother Dear	75
Elegy for The Old Farm House	76
Heaven is Family	77
Family Fig Tree	78
Seasons of Life	79
Papa Cole and Mama Cole	83
What's in a Name?	84
I Loved Her So!	85
Nephews in Flight	86
Family Is Forever	87
Celestial Rainbows	91
Kind Father	92
Our Inherited Responsibility—	93

Dedication

This book is a poetic memoir of the Robert Lewis and Jessie Pearl Cole family. Saint Augustine said that God loves each one of us as though each is the only one to love. My parents never read Augustine's Confessions, but they lived the truth of this faith statement. They daily loved each of their thirteen children as though each was the only one to love. This book is dedicated to them. Also, it could not have been written without the contributions of my family, especially Houston and Bonnie. Many submitted memories to me during the writing. A special thank you to them and to Tonya Jenkins Richey who took the barn photo on the front cover. Also special thanks to Randy Cole for calling my attention to the photo that has circulated among the family and is loved by all. However, I am responsible for the final shaping of those memories, and the book is my own poetic memoir.

> Mother and Daddy
> taught us inside every word
> kindness is waiting

> When a father tells the child a story,
> he becomes a father and a child.
> Both become one,
> listening together—
> To the wisdom of the ages.

Down on the Farm in Georgia

**Memories of The Family
of
Robert Lewis Cole
and
Jessie Pearl Stamps**

Family Data

Robert Lewis Cole was born on April 26, 1899
Jessie Pearl Stamps was born on February 15, 1908
Robert and Jessie were married on January 18, 1927

Their Marriage was blessed with 13 children:

Robbie Arlene (11-2-1925)
Herbert Lewis (12-26-28), deceased
Claude Ertail, called C. E., (7-15-1930), deceased
Betty Ann (7-4-1932), deceased
Houston Milford (5-11-1934)
Michael Lawrence (4-20-36)
Peggy Marie (3-12-1938), deceased
Dwayne (4-20-1940)
Charlotte Mae (1-17-1942)
Wendell Mason (3-8-1944)
Janice Diane (4-3-1946), deceased
Barry Dean (9-27-48)
Bonnie Sue (11-21-1950)

Introduction

This book, *Down on the Farm in Georgia*,
is a collection of stories,
presented largely in a poetic framework as a memoir.
I lived on the farm from birth until my last two years
of college and seminary. Everything since is **memory**.

Memory writing may be called
an anamnesis form of writing.
As acts of remembering, these stories and poems
are not strictly speaking historical.
Remembrance is seldom if ever "pure" facts.

In the anamnesis poetic form of writing,
the faithful telling of past stories bridges past and present.
What links the past and present,
creating a new future,
is the experienced presence of family in each new telling.

Poetry writing can add a sense of humor.
For example, you can imagine what a selfie
would look like if it were taken to show
what it was like to grow up on a farm
as the eighth of thirteen children, as I did.

 After serving for 50 years as a busy pastor in the south,
Beth and I moved to Anchorage, Alaska,
to help with our two grandchildren
while our daughter, Kim, and son-in-law, Ken,
started their busy medical practice

This move was like a breath of fresh air for me.
With freedom to write, this book,
Down on the Farm in Georgia,
began to evolve from the stories first told to our children,
Kim and Kevin, and then our grandchildren,
Cole and Clara.

Witnessing the beauty of nature in Alaska's mountains,
salmon streams, moose, bears, birds, wild flowers, and alpenglow
sunrises and sunsets, these poetic stories
that had long lived in my memory came to life.

Buck Creek

The meandering stream
flows through the hills of Northwest Georgia,
until it empties into the Little Tallapoosa River,
and eventually makes its way to the Gulf Shore.

The crystal clear stream is formed by many springs
that trickle from the rocky hills of Northwest Georgia.
The water is not only clear;
it is also cool even on the hottest days of summer.

It is a perfect stream for trout, bass, bream, and sun perch.
Its cool water makes it a favorite
gathering place on hot summer days,
especially for children and youth.

A swimming party at Buck Creek
was the highlight of the summer for the Cole clan.
The cool springs would often be filled
with watermelons on a hot summer day.

Robert was especially fond of Buck Creek.
As a young man he crossed the creek many times
traveling from his family's farm to the Stamps' family farm
to see one of the Stamps girls.

Actually, according to his yarns,
Robert had dated all six sisters,
from the oldest to the youngest;
and then he married the youngest, Jessie Pearl.

When asked about this unusual fact,
Robert just grinned and said,
"I kept going till I found one that would have me!
I guess Jessie was just too young to know the difference."

Robert was 27 and Jessie Pearl was eighteen
when they were married.
The history of the Cole family
in Northwest Georgia is tied up with Buck Creek.

In the mythic stories of many cultures,
streams are sacred place—
thin places where
heaven and earth meet.

Buck Creek was such a place for the Cole family,

A Tribute to Father

God had a plan on April 26, 1899—
A little boy was born to Franklin Joseph and Maude Jones Cole.
The journey of our earthly father was mapped out by our Heavenly Father.
We are so blessed that God chose this man to be our Daddy!
He worked hard and provided shelter, food, clothing,
and most of all love!!! Happy birthday Daddy!!
We will see you and Mama again one Glorious day!!!
 (Written by Bonnie Sue).

(I added this to Bonnie's tribute).

Daddy was a self-taught watch maker.
If he did not have the part he needed,
he made it.

He taught us—
Anything broken can be fixed.
Then he let us watch him fix it!

Daddy's gift to us was this—
He didn't tell us how to fix our lives;
He let us watch him live.

Proverbial wisdom unfolded,
What the child sees
The child does
What the child does
The child is.

Hugged Home

Our family grew up in a farmhouse
that had too few rooms
for a family with thirteen children.
It had a hallway, called a dogtrot,
in the middle that ran
from the large front porch to the back porch.

It was enclosed with doors.
As you entered the hallway from the front door,
there was a sitting room on the left
and on down the hallway there was a kitchen
and eating room on the left.

The kitchen had a door that opened to the back porch.
On the right side of the hall as you entered the front door
there were two large bedrooms,
the same size as the two rooms
on the left side of the hall.

When my dad bought the farm,
an elderly couple lived there.
It was adequate space for two people,
but it didn't have enough rooms for our family.
Girls claimed the first bedroom
and parents took the other one.

This meant, of course, no room for the boys.
We closed in half of back porch. It worked very well.
On a cold snowy night a few snow flakes would drift in
falling on the quilts mother piled on.
A small boy's delight!

Precious memories
memories that never fade
oh, how they linger
sneaking out of our eyes
and rolling down our cheeks
thrilling our souls.

When we heard mother
read aloud from the Bible, John 14,
"In my Father's house are many mansions,"
our ears perked up.
Would we have a room of our own one day?

To be sure, my life and faith were shaped in that house
and on that farm, as were all 13 of us.
Growing up on the farm gave us a sense of security
and love that has never left us.

When I was about ten years old I was playing with two of my cousins at my grandparents' house. My mother had told me to be sure and come home before dark, since I would be walking through the woods alone.
It was a well-known and well-trodden path
about one mile long.

As children will do, I forgot the time.
Suddenly it was almost dark,
so I hurriedly said good-bye
and struck out through the woods.

In the beginning I was brave and felt good.
Then it grew darker.
At the half-way point I crossed the little brook
I had spent many hours playing in—

Catching blue trout with red eyes,
minnows with little horns on their head,
and tadpoles. I caught so many tadpoles
that my brothers and sisters
gave me the nickname, "Tadpole."

When my son, Kevin, launched me and my new computer on to AOL, precursor to the internet, he chose tadpole as my "screen name." I was greatly affronted to find that the name was already taken, and the computer would not let us enter that name. I yelled into the computer, "I had that name when I was seven years old, 1947, in fact. Before the computer age," I added defiantly. The computer didn't hear me; it only said, "Choose another name."

Kevin said, "let's try tadpolejr." As an eleven-year old, Kevin was chuckling and enjoying this immensely---A lot more than I was! The computer flashed back instantly, "tadpolejr accepted. Welcome tadpolejr and have a good journey on the world-wide-web."

Well, back to my journey through the dark woods. Crossing the brook, I was beginning to feel smaller than a tadpolejr. And I had a half- mile to go. My world at the age of ten was smaller than the world-wide-web, but it was large enough to be inhabited by rattle snakes, an occasional wild bobcat, and tales of a wild man who lived in those woods. Like many mythical tales there was a kernel of truth in this one. Old Sam could be seen on the dirt roads carrying a tow sack full of soup bones he had gathered behind the meat market in town. He brought the bones to his shack in the woods along the creek, on the other side of my grandparents' house. There he boiled them in gallon cans on an open fire with vegetables he got from people's gardens.

It was told, mainly by older brothers trying to scare little brothers, that Old Sam often frightened little children he found in his woods. Of course I was thinking about Sam as I crossed the brook into utter darkness. I no longer felt brave. Every bush was alive and shaking and the leaves rattled from small animals scurrying about. Later in life I learned an African proverb that boldly states, "All things which make noise at the side of the path do not come down the path." This is a good proverb for seasoned sages, but meaningless to a frightened ten year old.

Besides, the noise I heard was coming down the path! There were definite footsteps ahead. Then I saw him coming down the path toward me! I froze in my tracks! My feet would not move, but my heart raced rapidly! Out of the darkness came a familiar voice, "Son, is that you." Images of monsters melted away in the sunshine of those family words. I recognized the voice of my father who had come to meet me. My father hugged me home!

This childhood experience shaped my life and faith. According to an Irish proverb, "What the child sees, the child does, What the child does, the child is." Because of my kind father and gentle, nurturing mother, I grew up finding it easy to believe that this universe has a cosmic face of love and inside every word kindness is waiting.

One of My First Memories: Doodlebug

One of my early memories
is of the day we moved
to that farm house in 1944.
I was just a 4 year old child.

While the truck was being unloaded,
I crawled under our new farm house
made from timber sawn from the farm.

The house was sitting on stone pillars
and open from all sides.
I crawled under the house
out of a sense of insecurity
and to hide from all the noise
and totally new surroundings.

What I remember
is Peggy, my six year old sister, crawled in looking for me.
You see, the way a large family survives
is that the older ones take care of the younger.
I found these little funnel like holes in the sandy soil.

I asked Peggy what they were,
and she said,
"I will crawl out and ask daddy
what the holes are."

Daddy said, "let's crawl under
and we will see."

Sitting by one of the holes
daddy hummed,
"This is a doodlebug hole."

Then taking a twig,
he began to gently move the twig
around in the bottom of the hole while singing,

"Doodlebug, Doodlebug,
come play with me."

And lo and behold
a little bug appeared
in the bottom of the hole.
He tenderly picked it up,
put it in my hand
and said, "This is a doodlebug."

We grinned from ear to ear.
Perhaps, this is my first memory
because to this day
the strongest memory I have of daddy and mother
is that they were kind and gentle.
They loved each of their thirteen children
as though they were the only one to love.

From that day on
if life as a growing child
became confusing and hectic
I crawled under that house
and amused myself by singing
the little doodlebug jingle.

And to this day,
that experience
is the key hole
 through which
I view the world.

Home Maternity Ward

My siblings and I, all thirteen of us,
Were born at home,
Delivered by the family doctor.

Even Bonnie Sue,
Born on November 21, 1950,
Was home delivered.

I remember as a ten year old,
Playing in the front yard
And hearing the cries of a new born baby.

I guess our parents felt
A baker's dozen was enough.
Or, we finally got it right, and no more needed!

Cole Family Barn

In folk lore
barns are mysterious places
where animals talk
and humanoids walk.

If the farm is a library
the barn is the party book.
Barns have souls,
and play social roles.

Swaying, singing, dancing
in barn ways
happy to be
free all their days.

Many creatures visit within the walls.
Talk when no human is in the stalls.
A humanoid sleeps in the feed room.
Shares the animal's food in blue moon.

Very gentle souls are barns.
Rent free they invite frightened souls
to come rest
and barn owls can build a nest.

In all kinds of weather
birds can stop in to preen a feather.
Or simply rest a while
before going another mile.

It is good to save our barns
and learn their ways.
Wisdom comes in enjoying the gifts
of farm barn days.

(By the way, Blue Moon,
second full moon in one calendar month,
is a good time to have a barn dance).

Part II

The barn on our farm
was so filled with activity
that it seemed to be alive—
Have a life of its own.

I expected some morning,
swaying my kerosene lantern
down the path from the farm house,
to find the barn packed up and gone—

Deeper into the woods
to rejoin the kindred trees
from which its boards
had been rough sawn.

Or, since it held such a high rank
in the scheme of farm success,
to reimagine itself
as a new manger scene—

christening the animals
and barn owls
as friends of the divine—
A savior if you will.

Part III

Two fuzzy owlets
have just emerged from eggs.
Looking like yellow yarn.

Mother owl is in the rafters
scowling down at me.

Eyes that could call forth
the demons of the Apocalypse,
say, "touch my babies
and I will peck your eyes out."

The barn sprite
wailed, "that is why
my right eye is missing."

With a beak that could open
a coke bottle,
I was convinced.

Joy of Fresh Cut Hay

Fresh cut hay
lies in rows
waiting to be rolled.

Sweet aromas abound
all around
like spices in deep sleep.

Cottontails scamper
with babies in jaws.
Calling, the sky is falling!

The sky is falling!
We must quickly find new cover,
find new homes.

Has anyone seen Keehar
or Dandelion?
Wisdom is needed.
The sky is falling!

Part II

Hay has so little to do.
With cottontails to entertain
and bumble bees too.

Gather the sunshine in its sheath
Sway in the gentle breeze
and dance with sparkling pearls in the dew. And even when mowed
to share its sweet aroma.

Coming at last
to sleep the long nights away
dreaming in the family barn.
Owls in the rafters,
cattle asleep in the stalls.
Oh the joys
of fresh cut hay!

Part III

Hauling hay is a lot sweeter
and farm work is a lot easier
when your pitchfork is a pencil
and you are in Alaska, 4,290 miles away
from the hot hay fields
Down on the Farm in Georgia.

Part IV

In heaven Herbert and C.E.
who dropped out of school
at the end of the great depression,
before entering high school,
to work on the farm,
punch each other and chuckle!

Cotton Picking

Cotton was a big cash crop
for farmers in Georgia
when I was growing up
in the 1940's to 1950's.

When daddy sold the cotton bales
We all got a new pair of shoes,
the only pair we had for school
and Church until the next year.

On my birthday, April 20,
we pulled off our shoes
and went barefooted on the farm,
and these foot-loose days lasted
until the first big frost or snow in early winter.

Our large family, with everyone picking, could pick
a bale of cotton a day—about 1200
pounds from field and about 500 pounds per bale
after seeds were removed at Eli's cotton gin.

Once our crop was picked
we hired out to pick for neighbors
who had fewer children,
or none like Lint Boyd.
If we worked hard we could
Pick about 100 pounds per person and make $1.00 each.

You literally picked your
fingers to the bone
and they would be bleeding
at end of the day.

When I went to seminary
in Louisville, Kentucky, in 1964
I met a cotton picking girl
from Brighton, Tennessee.

And we have picked through
life together for 54 years.
Have had tow sacks full of fun
Worth more than $1.00
per hundred pounds.

Especially the fun of children
and grandchildren.
They have more than one pair of shoes.
Telling this yarn is more fun than real cotton picking!

The Hammer Mill

Daddy and Houston installed a new hammer mill
to crush feed for livestock.
When they started it up it blew up.
There was a large wrench left in it at factory,
and the wrench hit Houston in the groin
and knocked him down.
Pieces of metal hit daddy.
No broken bones, only bruised.
Insurance carrier tried to get daddy
to sue the company.
Daddy replied, "Anybody can make a mistake."
Company came and set up a new one.
Stayed there to be sure it worked properly.

Sorghum Mill

Daddy was a firm believer in the old saying—
Idle hands are the devil's workshop.
He was always coming up with new farm projects,

especially ones to keep the boys busy.
We had a large fruit orchard
and caring for it required a lot of work,

not to mention cotton fields,
corn, and hay,
all to be gathered by hand.

Daddy said, Cathead biscuits
and home churned butter
needed sorghum syrup to be complete.

Went to Buck Creek
and gathered stone to make
sixteen feet long by four feet wide firebox
with stone chimney.

Had a copper pan made the same size.
Six inches deep to sit on the firebox.
Pan was divided into 24 eight inch sections

with openings on opposite sides
so the raw sorghum juice from mill
would flow in zig zag pattern
from one end to the other.

Houston, Michael, Wendell, Barry, and I
fed the sugar cane into the grinding mill,
hauled away the pulp,
and kept the fifty gallon wooden barrel full of juice.

A copper pipe with tap for closing and opening
came out of the bottom of the barrel
and carried the raw juice to the cooking pan.

As it flowed in the pan with hot fire under neath
from one end to the other
copper skimmers were used to dip pulp
that rose to the top as it was cooked.

there was a tapped spout to let the
cooked syrup flow into quart jars
that were put on a table to be boxed

Or just hold a fresh biscuit
delivered by mama,
Peggy, Charlotte, Janice, and Bonnie

under the drip spout
And rub rub your tummy!
Yum! Yum!

Old Gray Mules

On our working farm
we had stubborn gray mules.
One was named Bird.

Contemplating on an old stump,
the knot head mule
haunts me today.

Here is the rest of the story.

Daddy traded for two young mules
that were quite rotten
When Houston and C.E.
were planting cotton.

Ole Bird,
the mule Houston was using,
according to his yarn,
decided to go to the barn.

A hay rake was in the path,
and Ole Bird's big mistake
was jumping the tongue of the rake.

The cotton planter hit the tongue.
Flew into many pieces.
Houston fell down on the ground
and began to roll around.

Cursing the gray mule.
Crying,
but feeling lucky
to be alive.

He told Daddy
he didn't mind working hard,
but he wished
we had some tamer mules.

Part II

When daddy went to buy new mules
he spotted two old gray mares.

You don't want those,
the salesman said.

Why?

They go so slow
you think they are backing up.

Soon they will be back in the barn stall
not moving at all.

How much?
Just a few bucks.

Daddy grinned,
Load them on the truck!

Part III

One mule was so slow
you could get a drink of buttermilk
while she was turning around
at the end of a row.

Some of the reasons
Houston put farming down
and moved to town.

Blackberry Picking

Down on the farm in Georgia
Hot stones
Blackberry picking time
Fingers pricked
Chiggers itching time

Swamp blackberries
Big as your thumb
Hang on brambles
Along the creek banks
Blue trout dart
through crystal

spring fed waters
flowing over mill rocks
carved out of the centuries
Cherokee play ground

Mill grinding corn
Pone bread
Blackberry spread

Sweetness of summer abounds
Broiled trout
Happy days

Charlotte, Janice, and Bonnie
were champion berry pickers
They knew which ones would make the best
blackberry cobbler and jam

Free for all
Except for uncles and aunts
Who live in town
50 cents a pail for them
It's blackberry picking time!

Wild Plums

Down on the farm in Georgia
along abandoned red clay roads
wild plum trees grow.

Finding ripe
yellow and red plums—
hot July day delight.

Oh, the joy
of eating wild plums
fresh off the bush.

Spitting seeds
juice trickling down chin.
Then doing it again.

On the way to the mill rocks
Swimming in cool pools
Skirting water snakes.

Diving to spot
Red-eyed blue trout
with black dots.

Cutting a cane pole
tying line and hook
finding grasshopper.

Catching dinner
Cat head biscuits
Wild plum jelly!

Bobcat Byte

Exploring our farm alone one summer morning,
I discovered a cave
behind a fallen tree
that had lost its leaves.

I cautiously crawled inside without a light.
The cavern was as large as a bedroom
and as dark as a moonless midnight.

Something sprang from a ledge
as quick as a flash of light
and landed six feet in front of my feet.

My heart fluttered
As my eyes adjusted to the absence of sunlight,
I saw two glowing eyes looking so neat.

Stretching out furry paws,
quivering dappled jaws,
Soft as cotton paws

sent shivers down my spine.
Quietly I backed away,
and dove through the opening.

The dinner table conversation
was lively that night.
But no one of the baker's dozen believed
the story of bobcat byte.

Fall Farm Haiku

In the old farm pond
Beavers are having such fun
Water is lapping

It is early fall
Cattle are all in the stall
Barn owl eyeing mice

Plop, Sound of falling!
Watermelons grow on ground!
Old scarecrow falls down.

How they soothe me
Nighttime dreams of mom and dad
Warm my heart and soul

Whether sweet or sour
We do not know. This is first
Cherry picking day.

Hugs all around room
Dad says farewell to family.
Darkness falls on farm

Cool breeze parts curtains
Tears of sadness roll down cheeks
Sunrise brightens trees

Watching a sunset
Reclining on mountain side
Mother died last week

As we grow older
Sorrows mount like cold snow banks
Then the sun rises!

A child's first full moon
On the playroom floor dancing
Shadows of night owl.

A falling maple leaf
Wafts to and fro to the ground
It's a butterfly!

A falling red leaf
Wafts to and fro to the ground
It flies up again!

Rolling Country Store

Every Thursday a bus came rolling by our farm.
It was an old school bus painted blue.

On the sides were the words—
Rolling Country Store.

All the seats were ripped out
And shelves were added from floor to ceiling on both sides.

Then it was filled with basic grocery store items.
With lots of bottles of soda pop, candy, and ice cream.

With eagle eyes the small children
Watched the road and listened for the sound.

When it was spotted, the dinner bell was sounded
For those doing farm chores to come running.

All the children tried to keep enough coins
From blackberries sold and cotton picked for neighbors.

A nickel for cokes and small ice cream cups.
And lots of penny candy.

Oh, the delight!
Of the rolling country store!

Watermelon Thumping Time

A summer watermelon fest
is better than all the rest.

Watermelons contain
antioxidant lycopene

and amino acid citrulline
in the pink flesh and the rind.

Some research shows
that these natural ingredients

improve blood pressure
and cardiac stress.

Stress is further reduced
when watermelons are eaten

in social gatherings
like swimming in cool streams.

I grew up with my fingers and toes
planted in the soil of Georgia

where watermelon thumping to determine ripeness
was an art that parents would be sure to impart.

We took watermelons to swimming parties
on Buck Creek and

stashed them to cool
in a spring fed pool.

Buck creek flowed into
the Tallapoosa River.

Try saying that line
with a mouth full of watermelon rind.

listen to adults giggle
and punch each other.

Memories of thick slices melting
on sun-parched tongues and lips,

dribbling down chins
to belly buttons.

Thrill.
Still.

Memories of
holding the best part---

black bullet seeds,
to be spit at each other

in friendly battle,
like rapid gun fire.

And when the seeds
were not enough

we bombed each other
with the edible rinds.

Fortunately,
the amino acid in watermelons

protects against muscle pain.
Now, if this poem can do the same!

Dan and Alice

Dan and Alice lived
on one of our farms.
Dan's face wrinkled
from too much sun.

Hands calloused from holding
the wooden plow handles,
Tilling the clay soil
and planting crops.

The horn of plenty,
drank from a bitter cup.

For all, who like Dan and Alice,
defeated by race and prejudice,
Heaven received
as God's children.

Mercy,
Grace,
and peace.
Dan and Alice.

Part II

The preacher of the little weather beaten church
on Hog Liver Road
stands at attention
Grinding stones turning
Corn meal flowing from chute
Dan in sing-song rhythm
God sure is good
You can't out scoop God
The more you scoop up
The more comes your way!

Part III

One moonless midnight
A large natural gas pipe line exploded
rattling windows in farm houses for miles
Dan who had told us boys
that pajamas were made for putting
at the foot of the bed in case there was a fire
jumped out of bed
forgot his pajamas
and ran for a mile
down the red clay dirt road
before the roar of the explosion quieted
He ran back home
and found Alice still lying in bed
Dan asked her how she could stay in bed
when Gabriel was blowing his horn
and the end of the world was coming
Alice quietly said
Well he could take me lying in bed
easier that an old fool like you
running down the road butt naked
I don't guess Dan told that in his sermon on Sunday!

Part IV

Alice who had a heart of gold
was a large woman
She told us that she had the "dropsies"
laughing she said
I drop in every soft chair I pass
and stay for a long time!

(Dan and Alice are for real. I loved them dearly.
I still smile every time I think of them. They both
Had hearts of gold. They did not have children,
and they treated us like we were their own).

Goat Man

Charlotte, Wendell, Janice, and I were working in the garden
The girls were the keepers of the garden
They knew when the vegetables were ready to pick
How to prepare and cook them for best flavor
Wendell and I were talking rabbit boxes

We heard something rattling down
The red clay road in front of our farm house
We saw the strangest thing
A covered wagon pulled by about 30 goats

As it pulled in front of our house
We right away picked up the strong odor of goats
The man introduced himself as "Ches" the goat man
I guess if you live with goats
Your diet is mainly goat milk and goat cheese
You wear clothes made from goat skins
You will be called The Goat Man

He asked daddy if he could camp on our farm
Build a campfire to cook his meals
The old covered wagon had pots pans
Everything imaginable hanging on the sides
Daddy said that he could stay
Added we have plenty of fresh vegetables just picked
You won't have to cook your own meal

Mother and my sisters started cooking
    Fried chicken
        Corn on the cob
            Fried okra
                Black-eyed peas
                    Mashed potatoes—
                        Topped off with egg custard pies

The Goat Man said grace
        We all ate with gusto
                He said it was the best meal he ever had

After the meal the goat man
Entertained us for hours
He said that he was once beaten to death
But when the undertaker stuck an embalming needle in him
He jerked upright on the table
The funeral director almost died of fright

The goat man said that the near death experience
Sent him on the road as a traveling preacher
Came close to the fires of hell
It wasn't a place you wanted to go

He met a knife throwing circus artist
They got married
He became her target
Showed us a few scars

She traveled with him
Until she grew weary and left
We had a son
He traveled with me
Until he ran away one day
Some scars are on the inside and you can't see them

He sure knew how to tell a yarn
I have travelled in all the lower 48 states
Even got to Alaska
I would have gone to Hawaii
My goats couldn't swim that far
Besides they probably would have eaten the grass skirts
Off the hula dancers

After the goat man left our farm,
mother fired up the old cast iron pot
On the out-door fire
Filled the wash tubs with hot water
made us all strip off our clothes
We and our clothes got a good scrubbing

Probably a little over precautious
After all The Goat Man was hardly ever sick
Couldn't even be beaten to death
Lived to the ripe old age of 97

Gray Fox

Winter—
and the sky was gray.
Silver clouds
kept the sun at bay.

Michael and I
Packed an old army backpack
Gathered a few snacks
and other nicknacks

Hunting guns taken off the racks
Strapped snugly over our backs
Off to the woods we run
In pursuit of fun.

Alertly looking for some tracks.
Adventure hunting.
Never knowing where the next turn
would take us.

Scanning the trees for squirrels
for mama's stew pot
Something a little strange
caught my attention.

Twenty feet up this stubby red oak tree
eyes of fire were blazing down at me.
Gray fur barely visible
against a slate gray sky.

Shivering a little,
rattled even more,
I nudged Michael
my comrade in mischief.

Michael and I had skipped school.
I was twelve years old.
Michael, my idol,
four years, my senior.

I whispered
while pointing,
What is that?

Michael, named for an angel,
but far from it,
whispered back,

it looks like two foxes,
but it can't be.
Foxes are red, not gray,
and they don't climb trees.

In the same quiet tone—

You take the one on the left,
aim for the head,
I'll take the one on the right.
both will be dead.

On the count of three!
Boom! Boom!

Back in the farm house,
mamma heard the shots
echoing off the weathered gray barn.
Got the stew pot hot.

Picking up our bounty,
I felt my heart pounding,
a wild thing,
small and full of meanness.

My mind hiding
from those eyes—
Fire eyes still open,
singing a death song.

Grinning through rows
of picket fence teeth
the sly faces seemed to say,
Why did you do this to us?

We were only hoping
to catch a few rays
of early morning sun
after a night of frolicking fun.

Why?
Yes, indeed, why?
The mind often lags behind
the excitement of the moment.

These gray foxes
were an oddity—
definitely not meat
for the stew pot.

Only furs to hang
on the side of the barn
As a warning to all foxes—
Singing a death song.

Leave our chickens alone!

Why indeed?

Sixty-six years later,
as I write this adventure,
the question still haunts me.

Life on the farm
as the middle of thirteen children
was sometimes rough

as the corn cobs
we used in fights
with neighborhood boys—

Singing the death song.
Slaughtering hogs and cows for
bacon and burgers

was not a gentle chore.
Memories of those days have
nearly made me want meat no more.

Fox Limerick

Once there was a sly old gray fox
Who was fond of bagel and lox
Visited Alaska
Had lox thereafter
For good lox he would shadow box

Gathering Honey

For Herbert and C. E.,
no challenge went unmet.

They would find
and climb the honey tree.

Plenty of bees buzzing
    sipping nectar.

They would just
follow them to the honey tree.

Climb and eat chunks
of pure golden delight.

Honey fresh from the hive fills you
with the essence of fruit blossoms.

Heaven could be no purer
than honey, the nectar of the gods!

Part II

Houston
four years younger than C. E.

Helped rob the honey trees
Would soak rags in sulfur

Build a fire in base of tree
Put soaked rags on fire

The smoke would stun the bees
long enough to get the honey comb

Part III

Cousin Walter

Kept a paddle in his back pocket
Good for swatting bees
That made it out of the sulfur smoked tree
To rid themselves of the odor
They would all take a dip in Little Creek

Walter was known for pulling down wasps nest
Swatting the wasps with his paddle
He kept in his back pocket
On the way to the creek
Walter noticed a big wasp nest in a bush
He walked over
Gave the bush a good shaking
Reached for the paddle in his back pocket

It was not there
He had lost it on the way to the creek
So many wasps stung him
He swelled real bad
Sore for days

Herbert
    C. E.
        Houston
            Didn't get stung
                Probably outran the wasp
                    Dived under the water

Spearing White Suckers

On our farm in late April,
white suckers ran up the streams
to build spawning beds in the riffles.

Wading up the creeks,
with spears sharpened,
you could hear them splashing.

Leaping with delight,
ripping the riffles to shreds,
tumbling upon each other.

Witnessing such a frenzy,
it was hard to know
where imagination ends
and reality begins.

(Wendell and Barry, my two youngest brothers,
were good at catching the suckers by hand
and tossing them in a cotton picking tow sack
worn on the back).

Cherished Memories

Some of my most cherished memories
are seeing my mother
and grandmother, Maude Cole,
sitting in their rockers
with open Bible in lap
each night before going to bed.

The radiance of their smiles
still shine for me.
Their heart of faith beats in me,
and the warmth of their soul
is my daily sunshine.

I also remember their tender touch-
Cathead biscuits
Kind words
Angel glow.

Chickens

Like the Senator from Georgia,
John Lewis,
I grew up on the farm
caring for our flock of chickens,
feeding them cracked corn
and food scraps.

I, along with my six brothers
and six sisters,
was taken to Church from birth.
I was captivated by the preacher.

So, naturally, while feeding
my flock of chickens,
I would sometimes preach to them.

One Sunday morning, dressed in my
short pants and tee shirt,
waiting for everyone to get ready for church,
which was quite a chore,
I went out to deliver my sermon.

Seeing the cute little biddies,
I stooped to pick one up and
held it tenderly to my cheek.
The mother hen was not impressed.

She betrayed my trust.
With rage she flogged me.
Her sharp beak drew blood on my leg.

I ran into the house screaming
bloody murder.

Michael, No Angel, teased me saying,
scare-ty cat, scare-ty cat,
Tadpole is afraid of a mother hen.

Mother stepped in
stopping the tussle,
and delivered the sermon before church—
Bathed my leg in water
and applied tender balm.

I kept the lessons learned in my heart,
to be brought out later when caring
for my church flock for fifty plus years.

Chasing Fireflies

As the sun sets
and stars begin to appear
in the sky,

A child can only wink
and smile.

Then into the child's world
fireflies begin to swirl.

Swirling, swirling swirling.
Emulating the spinning stars.

Though not stars at heart
Fireflies are happy to play the part.

The child is happy
With the night time art.

Tadpole

I am the eighth of thirteen children
and the only one without a middle name.

At least my parents
never got mad at me!

This made for a lot
of fun and games.

I was forever given
funny names---

There was one
that wiggled in

between my first name, Dwayne
 and my last name, Cole.

Tadpole
Dwayne Tadpole Cole.

True to its shape,
this little comma caused a pause—

Is your middle name
really tadpole?

Yep, I played in the little branch
that ran through our farm

and caught tadpoles
 by the dozens.

Kept them in fruit jars
on my dresser.

Watched them sprout legs
and hop from the jars.

All through the night little frogs
croaked through our farm house.

Until Papa said, No more tadpoles
can come into this house.

Then he added,
as an after thought—

That doesn't include you, Tadpole.
This will always be your home.

After leaving home for college
I learned---

Tadpole was the name
of a laptop computer.

Wow! I secretly thought.
A computer has been named after me.

Later I learned in a cosmology class
there is a Tadpole Galaxy.

Double Wow!
Get out of here!

A Galaxy
has been named after me.

The Tadpole Galaxy
is located

420 million light-years distance
toward the constellation, Draco.

Its eye-catching tail
is about 280 thousand light-years long

with massive,
bright blue star clusters.

I reported these facts
to my brothers and sisters with the tag line,

I demand more respect from you
in the future.

My middle name is Tadpole.
And don't try to wiggle out of it!

When I signed on to aol for email,
I chose tadpole as my screen name.

The message
quickly came back.

Already taken,
choose another.

What! I yelled at the computer.
How can that be?

I have had that middle name for many a year.
Computer did not hear.

Choose
another screen name.

My son, Kevin,
chuckled and said,

try tadpolejr, all small letters
in keeping with its size.

It was accepted and I was
taken down several notches.

Front Porch

Sitting on the Front Porch
Across from the hollow
Formed by Little Creek
Feeling so lucky
Filled with love
Being together
Where they belong
You are the music
The notes of my song
All my words
To you belong

Part II

Front porches are special places
in the rural South
A gathering place for uncles and aunts
Charlotte had this brilliant idea—
Let's crawl under the porch and sing
for our city family
The two of us sang
Maybe we are ragged and funny
and we ain't got a lot of money
Just traveling along
singing a song
side by side.

Uncle Jimmy got the message
and dropped coins though the cracks
in the porch floor.
Charlotte and I were ready
to take the show on the road!

Part III

Charlotte really was smart.
She was chosen as the best student
from her school class
to represent her class at the county fair.
I got to go along with her as big brother.
In payment I had to do many
of her cleaning chores for the next week.
The county fair was an exciting event in those days
with trapeze artists and lion tamers,
not counting all the fun rides.

Wendell's Rabbit Boxes

I remember running
the rabbit box route

with Wendell and Barry
before going to school.

If left in the boxes all day
the rabbits would try to chew out.

If we caught more than we could eat
we sold them for a treat.

Wendell has strong rabbit box skill
Making them for family still.

Randy was recently thrilled as Aesop
to get a box from Uncle Wendell's shop.

Wendell and Barry could keep pace
Slow and steady wins the race.

Sunday

After six working days on the farm,
Sunday was a welcome relief.
No picking cotton or pulling corn.
No mowing, raking, and hauling hay to the barn.

Just put on your Sunday best,
and go to church with all the rest.
Leave your old dirty words behind,
and new heavenly language find.

Hug all your friends once,
and hug some again and again.
If God was busy with the minister,
you might even sneak a kiss or two.

But the preacher said,
God has an all-seeing eye
that never blinks or closes in sleep.
That's the bleepity-bleep!

After worship,
tables were taken outside.
Food was spread far and wide.
Fried chicken, okra, corn on the cob.

Best of all,
mom's apple pie.

Back at home all the adults
settled down for a Sunday nap.
Even God was ready for a nap,
After all the preacher's yapity-yap.

With a sugar high
from all the 'cream and pie,
the children were ready
to play under the blue sky.

Rules were still aplenty
and we were not to forget any.
But since even God was fast asleep,
we broke a few, but not many.

For there was The Judgement Day!

Grandmother

My grandmother Maude Cole
died on December 26, 1964.
As young teenagers Michael and I spent
many weekends with her,
as did Charlotte and Janice,
Wendell, Barry, and Bonnie,
so she could stay in her family home
on the weekends.
The sweetness of her life
still lives with me.
The glory of her love
warms my heart
on this cold day in Alaska
as I write down these memories.
I can still see her reading her Bible
to me before going to bed.
Each word a tender earthly touch
of our Eternal God shaping our lives.
(I could say the same
for my dear mother)
Thank you grandmother.
In God's providence I was home
from seminary and with her
on the day she went
to be with God in heaven.
God is good
and meets each event
in our lives with kindness.

Grandfather Cole

Lover of Native American artifacts
collected arrowheads and relics far and wide
Visited by distant Cherokee relative,
Chief Eagle Feathers,
from Cherokee Reservation in North Carolina
Teller of vivid stories around campfires
Went to the great teepee in the sky
while I was just a kid
Wish you could have stayed longer
in this happy hunting ground!

VW Beetle Drives Away

I will never forget the day,
the VW beetle
packed with all my worldly belongings
drove away from the old farm house.

In my lap
was a Louisville map,
seminary information
stamped in my imagination.

All the way
through towns small and large
that old farm house
held sway.

I remember those last few moments
mom and dad standing
on the front porch waving goodbye
tears of pride cheering me on.

Memories of mother's tears
and father's warm embrace
would hold me
all through the years!

And become the key hole
    through which
        I view my life
            and the world.

The Day Daddy Died

The day daddy died,
I felt like a bird that no longer
had a tree to land in during a storm.

I felt the same on the day
mother passed away.

They are not gone you know.
The dead are not apart from the living;

They keep coming around every day,
in our words, in our ways,
singing joyfully about what lies ahead!

Families are forever!
Love is here to stay!

Mother, the Sweetest of All

I remember
how you would wear aprons
made from flower sacks
and stand at the stove
making my favorite cat head biscuits with sawmill gravy—
you know, the way only you
could make them.
Some were buttered
and filled with fig preserves
that were out of this world.
To this day, no one
can hold a candle to your biscuits
that you rolled out
by the dozens every day.
Your hands were
almost always cooking
or cleaning clothes in lye detergent
made in an old cast iron pot
in the back yard.
You had so many pots and pans.
13 children, oh my Gosh!
You had your own cooking school
with 6 daughters.
And you taught them well.
I can see the love
you shared with all of us.
Thank you for your tough tender ways.
Love you, Mama.
I can still smell your apron.
Mainly— I can feel you in my smile.
I Love you and long
for your gentleness still!

Heaven is Family

I may be far away
tending to my own,
but this will always
be my home.

Family is for ever
and not measured
in miles.

I miss those who
have gone on to heaven.
Yet they are with me every day
in loving ways.

For heaven is not far away,
and time is not
measured in years.

Heaven is in our joys,
in our imagination,
and in our tears.

Heaven is family.
Families are forever.

Robbie, Mother Dear

As the oldest child in our large family,
Robbie took on the mothering role very early,
as did Betty Ann and Peggy.

In a large family the older ones take care of the younger.
I would say Robbie kept Herbert and C. E., out of trouble,
but that would be going too far.

No one could do that.
But I would say she had a big role
in shaping their character.

This was in spite of the teasing all three received at school.
Claude Ertail was teased about his middle name.
After he came home from school crying

from children making fun of his middle name,
it was shortened to C. E.
As tough farm kids they soon put a stop to the teasing.

After mother's death,
in addition to caring
for her children, Edwin and Edie,
and their growing families

Robbie increased her caring
for the Cole clan.
From opening her home
for family gatherings,

to organizing contributions
for flowers for all occasions,
to calling people
on their birthdays.

Robbie will be 92 on November 2, 2019,
so that mothering role was graciously
taken by Bonnie and Edie a few years ago.

Elegy for The Old Farm House

We wear the cloak of sadness
walking around the ruins,
remembering with love
the old farm house.

No one announced
the time of her demise,
she just put on her funeral dress
and clothed herself in fire!

Great eternal gifts
our parents left us!
Tender words served up,
with every Sunday dinner.

Each evening we sat
on the foot-worn floor,
mother sitting in her rocker
smiling into her Bible.

Blessings emblazoned
each word aglow
as warm as the fire
In the wood burning stove.

Though we were farmyard tough
we were gentled by
washboard wrinkled hands
dripping with love.

Now the old farm house is gone---
went up in Ezekiel's chariot of fire
to join mamma and daddy
and the rest of family in heaven.

Heaven is Family

We miss our family who
have gone on to heaven.
Yet they are with us every day
in loving ways.

For heaven is not far away,
not measured in years.
Heaven is in our joys,
and in our tears.

Heaven and earth
are not separate realities.
Heaven is family.
Family is forever.

Family Fig Tree

Near the Southeast corner
of the old farm house
sprawls a fig tree
where it catches the first rays
of the morning sun.

Around the roots,
some as old as the farm house,
new suckers grow
it is the law of the land
to let them stand.

Growing like the Cole clan
to bear fruit for the drying pan.
Hot biscuits and fig preserves are a treat
very hard to beat.

Now the old farm house is gone
put on her funeral robe
and went up like Ezekiel's
fiery chariot in a cloud of smoke.

The shadowy family fig tree remains
spreading out new branches
where two doves can often be heard
cooing love songs as old as Eden.

Seasons of Life

As children we lived
in a large loving family
on a beautiful farm
in Northwest Georgia.

The smell of fruit trees
blooming in spring.
Bees buzzing
and butterflies flitting.

Homemade peach ice cream
and watermelon parties
with juice dribbling down chins
on warm summer evenings.

Riding on a wagon
of fresh cut hay in the fall.
Mama's cathead biscuits
filled with syrupy fig preserves all winter.

Changing seasons
bring intense pleasures.
Green leaves followed
by spinning golden things.

We experience the seasons
of farm life once in childhood.
Everything after that
is magical memory!

Part II

Today I sit in my recliner
79 years have come and gone.
Why should I try to remember?
How can I forget?

Responses from Extended Family

Papa Cole and Mama Cole

My sweet sweet Papa Cole
and Mama Cole,

Love for them so grand.
I'm grateful to be a part of their clan.

I have a family that is like gold.
Blessed am I to be in this fold.

Once I had their hands to hold.
Forever will they be deep within my soul.

(Written by Debbie Hudson,
daughter of Wendell and Brenda Cole,
Granddaughter of Robert and Jessie Cole)

No one loved their children and grandchildren
more than Granddaddy and Grandmother Cole.
They also loved beautiful birds,
and we were taught not to harm the birds.
I am sure they would love Debbie's red bird haiku:

Songs so beautiful
Leaves of green where red birds sing
Loved ones are so near

What's in a Name?

I put great importance on the Cole name
and I am proud of our heritage and history.
 From a very humble and meager beginning
arose a tremendous family that was taught
the important things in life are
first a Love for the Lord and then a love for family.
As a boy growing up I experienced these first hand.
The family gatherings on Sunday afternoons
after a time of worship were filled with children playing
while parents sat on that old front porch
and talked of things from church
to running rabbit boxes on Buck Creek.
Through the years families have a way of separating
through different circumstances,
but I am glad our family has remained relatively close.
I love each of you and again,
I am so proud to be a part of this great family.
I realize I have been very vocal on certain political
and religious topics the past few months
and my intent is not to create arguments,
but simply to express ideas
that are true and dear to my heart.
Things I believe in deeply.
I encourage anyone to have deep convictions
in what they believe and to be willing to stand
for those as Christ taught in his teachings.
At the same time it is important to have a spirit of love
and consideration of others.
Maybe the whole problem with the world today
is that we don't build rabbit boxes
or sit on the porch and watch the kids play.
(Ricky Cole, son of Herbert and Clarice Cole,
Grandson of Robert and Jessie Cole).

I Loved Her So!

Something that keeps recurring over and over in my memory
is that every time I visited grandma Cole,
she wanted me beside her.
Of course I was happy being anywhere she was.
I remember we had beauty shop day
at Betty Ann's house one Tuesday.
Robert was little but he wanted to go too and of course,
I would never leave him with anyone
except Barry and Fredia or Charlotte.
Charlotte was there too.
Betty Ann made lunch for all of us
and grandma Cole had her hair done.
But while we were there, of course,
I was right there with her doing her nails.
Betty Ann asked her if she liked having her nails done.
I told Betty Ann that of course she did.
She was a woman above all else
and even though she never said so,
she enjoyed being pampered.
So many wonderful memories
from a loving God fearing mother to us all.
 I loved her so.

(Patricia Reid, Wife of Stephen Reid,
daughter-in-law of Peggy and Chester Reid).

Nephews in Flight

No matter how big the family grew,
Grandpa still insisted that
each family gathering had to be
at the old farm house.

The aged pear tree
out by the pump house
was worn smooth by children
climbing in it.

It had two limbs that formed a seat
that you could sit in
with two steering knobs
coming out of a dash.

Snoopy had his dog house
Cousins had a cockpit in pear tree.
Randy, Ricky, Tony, Keith
and others would sit there

and pretend that it was an airplane;
and they flew that plane
around the world
and back many times.

That imaginary plane carried them
Into successful careers.
It flew Tony all the way
through medical school.

(This memory, with exception of last verse
belongs to Randy Cole)

Family Is Forever

We miss members of our family who
have gone on to heaven.
Yet they are with us every day
in loving ways.

For heaven is not far away,
not measured in years.
Heaven is in our joys,
and in our tears.

Heaven is family.
Family is forever.

Conclusion

Celestial Rainbows

As I write this final chapter in May, 2019,
Mother and Daddy, Herbert and C. E.,
Betty Ann, Janice, and Peggy

are already in heaven painting celestial rainbows
brushed with angel wings
Splashed with all the colors of heaven.

A personal rainbow for each of us
to hang in the window of our soul.
So each new day can radiate

love energy from our celestial family
opening new dimensions of
promise, security, and hope.

Thank you, dear loved ones,
for this wondrous work!
Gifts from the celestial realm!

Kind Father

I see daddy standing with the saints in heaven
as he stood on Sunday in our little country church
praying, "Kind Father.

"Kind Father, watch over our growing family on earth."
Kindness shown to family
is the most healing force in the world.

All the saints in heaven join in singing.
"The Lamb in the center of the throne
will be your shepherd.

"You will be led to streams of life-giving water
and God will wipe
all tears from your eyes" (Based on Revelation 7:17).

I look and behold I see in heaven
Grandmother Cole and Mama
sitting side by side
with open Bibles in their laps

Reading in unison—

The Lord is my shepherd.
I will never be in need.
I rest in green pastures
and beside streams of peaceful waters.
My life is refreshed.
You lead me in the right paths.
I walk through dark valleys,
but I won't be afraid.
You are with me.
Your shepherd's rod makes me feel safe.
I sit at your banquet table and feast
on your kindness and love.
I will live forever
in your house, Lord (Based on Psalm 23).

Our Inherited Responsibility—

We, the Robert and Jessie Cole family,
have an inherited responsibility
to receive what we have been given,
polish it like silver heirlooms,
and use it for the blessing of our heirs
and for the good of all.

I have kept many of mama and daddy's
pearls of wisdom,
tucked them into
the pockets of my soul,

and brought them out for guidance
in my times of need.

Here is a sparkling jewel from daddy:
Learned from his farming days
and polished in watch repair shop ways—

Anything broken can be fixed.
Including broken hearts.

The strength of our families is
testimony to this time honored
inherited responsibility.

You can tuck this jewel from daddy,
polished by mamma, into your watch pocket,
apron pocket, or iPad,
as a Pearl of wisdom.

And each of you, my beloved family,
have some jewels tucked in your soul.
Bring one out into the light and share it
with everyone in our blessed family.

This book is my spiritual memoir,
my memories that became the key hole

through which I view life.
They are stories I told Kim and Kevin, Cole and Clara.
I hope in reading them
they will reflect some memories of all the family
and inspire the sharing of other memories within each family.

Goodness and kindness
has filled our lives.
How can we forget
All the light that illumines our days?

Knitted in our genes
In our flesh and bones
are precious gifts—The seasons of Eternity!

Other Books by Dwayne Cole

A Center that Holds: Adventures in Kindness.

A Prayer of Blessing: As You Go Remember This.

A Relational Hermeneutic of Kindness.

A Relational Trinity of Kindness.

Gentle Galilean Glories: The Tender Teachings of Jesus

God and Evil: An Ode to Kindness.

Jesus' Transforming Beatitudes: Selected Sermons from Year A.

Jesus' Transforming Love: Selected Sermons from Year B.

Jesus' Transforming Gentle Teachings: Selected Sermons from Year C.

Poems Inspired by Process Philosophy

The Apostles' Creed: A Living Creed for the Living Church.

The Book of Revelation: Jesus' Kindness Transforms Suffering.

The Serenity Prayer: A Pathway to Peace and Happiness.

The Story of the Bible: Authority, Inspiration, Canonization, and Translation.

Trees and Driftwood: Poetic Ecology

www.ingramcontent.com/pod-product-compliance
Lightning Source LLC
Chambersburg PA
CBHW052202110526
44591CB00012B/2048